TIME TRAVELING TO
1954

CELEBRATING A SPECIAL YEAR

TIME TRAVELING TO 1954

Author

David J. Anderson

Design

Gonçalo Sousa

November 2023

ISBN: 9798870058504

Surprise!

Dear reader, thank you so much for purchasing my book!

To make this book more (much more!) affordable, the images are all black & white, but I've created a special gift for you!

You can now have access, for FREE, to the PDF version of this book with the original images!

Keep in mind that some are originally black and white, but some are colored.

Go to page 101 and follow the instructions to download it.

I hope you enjoy it!

Contents

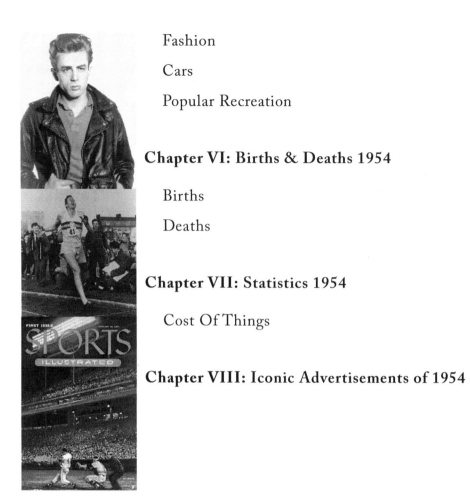

Chapter I: News & Current Events 1954

Leading Events

Monroe & DiMaggio: Hollywood's Star-Studded Union - January 14th

Marilyn Monroe with Joe DiMaggio

The romance between Marilyn Monroe, Hollywood's luminary, and Joe DiMaggio, the baseball legend, was as brief as it was fervent. Their whirlwind courtship led to a wedding that captured the public's imagination, but the fairy tale ended just nine months later with a divorce that captured headlines. Monroe, whose allure had initially enchanted DiMaggio, found herself at odds with his desire for privacy and normalcy, clashing with her own vibrant persona and public life.

The strains in their relationship came to a head when Monroe, besieged by cameras, announced their separation, marking an indelible moment of sorrow and sensation. Despite the split, Monroe's star continued to rise as she delivered performances that solidified her status as an icon. However, her personal life remained tumultuous, leading to more heartache and ultimately, her tragic and premature death.

Marriage Day

In the years following their divorce, DiMaggio re-entered Monroe's life, offering support during her most vulnerable moments and even proposing a second walk down the aisle. His steadfast presence during her final years hinted at a lingering bond between the pair. Yet, her passing at the age of 36 left DiMaggio bereft, a man who carried the torch for his lost love till the end of his days, never choosing to marry again. Their storied romance remains a poignant chapter in the annals of Hollywood's history.

Congress Greenlights Air Force Academy in Colorado – April 1st

The vision for an exclusive academy to shape the future leaders of the U.S. Air Force, parallel to the Army's West Point and the Navy's Annapolis,

finally materialized with congressional approval in 1954. The realization of this dream had been in the works since Lieutenant Colonel A.J. Hanlon's 1918 advocacy for an Air Service academy, but it wasn't until the post-World

U.S. Air Force Academy under construction

War II era that the concept gained significant momentum.

The establishment of an independent Air Force in 1947 through the National Security Act underscored the need for a dedicated training ground. This led to President Eisenhower's endorsement of the U.S. Air Force Academy, with its location carefully chosen by a committee that included aviation icon Charles Lindbergh and Air Force stalwart General Carl Spaatz.

Colorado Springs was selected from over five hundred candidates to host the academy, a decision driven by strategic considerations and the area's natural beauty. The U.S. Air Force Academy has since evolved into a premier military training institution, esteemed for its rigorous academic and military programs. It serves as a testament to America's enduring commitment to dominating the skies and, more recently, space, cultivating generations of officers who exemplify air and space power.

Historic Court Decision: U.S. Schools Pivot to Change - May 17th

Front page of The New York Times, announcing
the Supreme Court decision

For six decades before the seminal "Brown v. Board of Education of Topeka" ruling, the U.S. was entrenched in racial segregation, reinforced by the Supreme Court's endorsement in "Plessy v. Ferguson" (1896) which supported "separate but equal" facilities. However, not all states were uniform in their approach, with 17 enforcing segregation and 16 prohibiting it. Starting in the 1930s, NAACP and Howard University scholars aimed to challenge this by targeting graduate school segregation. Successful cases like "Sweatt v. Painter" (1950) set the stage by highlighting the inherent inequality of segregation. Oliver Brown's case argued that so-called "equal" segregated schools perpetuated subpar conditions

Lawyers celebrating the victory outside the U.S. Supreme Court, Washington, D.C.

for Black Americans. The court's deliberation was influenced by global perspectives, such as UNESCO's 1950 anti-racism declaration "The Race Question", and Gunnar Myrdal's critique in "An American Dilemma". Amid the Cold War, U.S. international standing was under scrutiny due to its racial policies. Questions about America's commitment to human rights arose globally, with figures like Justice William O. Douglas being confronted about racial injustice during foreign visits. Chief Justice Earl Warren, recognizing the geopolitical implications, emphasized the importance of America upholding its Constitution's principles. The unanimous "Brown" decision signaled a pivot, challenging the deeply entrenched racial divisions and setting the nation on a path toward integration.

'On The Waterfront': Brando's Rise to Oscar Glory - July 28th

The 1954 American crime drama "On The Waterfront" cemented its place in cinematic history with a gripping portrayal of union corruption along the

docks of New Jersey. With Elia Kazan's
direction and Budd Schulberg's script,
Marlon Brando delivered an Oscar-
winning performance that defined
his career. Alongside him, Eva Marie
Saint made a memorable film debut.
Inspired by real-life investigations into
waterfront crime, the film diverged from
Malcolm Johnson's original Pulitzer-
winning series to offer a narrative that
resonated deeply with audiences.
The film's cultural impact was undeniable,
reaping eight Academy Awards from
twelve nominations, including Best
Picture. Leonard Bernstein's evocative

On the Waterfront

score marked a unique foray into film composition, contributing to the movie's
enduring legacy. "On The Waterfront" was later honored by the U.S. National
Film Registry for its significance in American film history.

Yet, the movie's release was not without controversy. It reflected director
Kazan's personal politics, serving as an allegory for his own experiences with
the House Committee on Un-American Activities. The project initially saw

collaboration
with playwright
Arthur
Miller, but his
departure due to
Kazan's actions
led Schulberg to
step in.

Marlon Brando and Eva Marie Saint

The character Johnny Friendly, menacingly portrayed in the film, was drawn from the notorious real-life figure Johnny Dio, known for his criminal activities in labor racketeering.

East Coast in Turmoil: Hazel's Rampage Strikes - October 15th

Hurricane Hazel stands as one of the deadliest and most intense storms of the 1954 Atlantic hurricane season. Originating in Haiti, it caused the tragic deaths of 469 people and decimated the nation's coffee and cacao crops. Its terror didn't stop there; Hazel roared into the U.S., making landfall near the North-South

Hurricane Hazel's impact in Crisfield

Carolina border as a formidable Category 4 hurricane.

The storm claimed 95 lives in the U.S., before heading north to Canada, where it struck Toronto particularly hard, causing severe flooding and raising the death toll by another 81 lives.

This unprecedented storm caught many off-guard, with Toronto bearing the worst due to prior heavy rainfall and a general underestimation of the storm's residual power over land. As Hazel merged with a cold front, it astonishingly retained its intensity, even appearing as powerful as a Category 1 hurricane over

It destroyed parts of North Carolina

Toronto. The aftermath saw a mobilization of 800 military personnel for cleanup and a Hurricane Relief Fund established to distribute aid.

Sadly, by the time Hazel had dissipated, it left in its wake vast destruction, countless homeless, and a combined economic damage exceeding hundreds of millions in both U.S. and Canadian dollars.

Other Major Events

Hernandez Victory: Boost for Mexican American Rights - May 3rd

Gus Garcia represented Pete Hernández in Hernández vs. Texas

The U.S. Supreme Court's decision in Hernandez v. Texas marked a pivotal advancement for Mexican American civil rights. It unanimously declared that Mexican Americans were entitled to the same constitutional protections as other groups under the 14th Amendment.

At the heart of the case was Peter Hernandez, convicted of murder by an all-white jury from which Mexican Americans had been systematically excluded for over a quarter-century.

The defense highlighted the stark discrimination, showing no Mexican American had served on a jury in Jackson County for 25 years, despite many being eligible. Texas argued that Mexican Americans were classified as white and therefore not a distinct group under the 14th Amendment. However, Hernandez's lawyers demonstrated pervasive discrimination, from segregated schools to public bias against Mexican Americans, proving an unspoken exclusion policy.

Chief Justice Earl Warren's written opinion clarified that the 14th Amendment's protections were not confined to racial binaries but extended to any discriminated nationality group. The Court's decision recognized the specific challenges faced by Mexican Americans, propelling the Civil Rights Movement forward by broadening its inclusivity. This case not only reinforced the legal standing of Mexican Americans but also set a precedent for safeguarding the rights of all ethnic groups within the United States.

J. Robert Oppenheimer at the Guest Lodge

Oppenheimer Sidelined: Politics and Science Clash – May 6th

J. Robert Oppenheimer, fundamental in developing the atomic bomb, faced a stark clash between his scientific achievements and the era's political climate. His leadership at the Manhattan Project's Los Alamos Laboratory was instrumental in the Trinity test and the consequent bombings that ended World War II. However, his post-war advocacy for nuclear disarmament and opposition to the hydrogen bomb's development brought him into conflict with government and military officials. Oppenheimer's involvement with the Communist Party USA and his stance on nuclear policy led to the revocation of his security clearance in 1954, amidst the intense anti-communist sentiment of the second Red Scare. This decision effectively barred him from further contributions to nuclear physics and diminished his influence within political circles.

Despite this setback, Oppenheimer continued his academic pursuits, including a leadership role at Princeton's Institute for Advanced Study.

Oppenheimer Security Hearing

It wasn't until the Enrico Fermi Award in 1963 that his political reputation began to recover. After his death, the government posthumously reinstated his clearance in 2022, correcting the historical record and acknowledging the complexity of his legacy. This act served not only as a belated recognition of Oppenheimer's scientific contributions but also as a reflection on the period's political dynamics that once overshadowed his career.

Pledge of Allegiance: 'Under God' Added - June 14th

The Pledge of Allegiance, a staple of American patriotism, saw its most significant change with the addition of "under God." This alteration reflected the Cold War's ideological battle, as the U.S. sought to define itself against atheistic communist ideologies. The phrase's adoption was propelled by the socio-political landscape and a desire to underscore the nation's spiritual foundations. The concept was first proposed by Louis A. Bowman in 1948, influenced

Words, 'Under God,' Inserted In Pledge of Allegiance

Washington, June 14 (AP)—President Eisenhower signed today a bill inserting the words "Under God" into the pledge of allegiance to the flag, and said in a statement this will strengthen the "spiritual weapons which forever will be our country's most powerful resource."

A short time later, American Legion officials raised a new flag on the Capitol steps to mark Flag Day, and joined in the first official recitation of the revised pledge.

The flag raised to the top of the pole in front of the Capitol dome, was presented by the Legion. Rep. Rabaut (D-Mich), sponsor of the bill, and Sen. Ferguson (R-Mich), led the group in reciting the pledge.

As he signed the bill, Eisenhower issued this statement:

"From this day forward the millions of our school children will daily proclaim in city and town, every village and rural school house, the dedication of our nation and our people to the Almighty. To anyone who truly loves America, nothing could be more inspiring than to contemplate this school morning, to our country's true meaning.

"Especially is this meaningful as we regard today's world. Over the globe, mankind has been cruelly torn by violence and brutality and, by the millions, deadened in the mind and soul by a materialistic philosophy of life. Man everywhere is appalled by the prospect of atomic war.

"In this way we are reaffirming the transcendence of religious faith in America's heritage and future; in this way we shall constantly strengthen those spiritual weapons which forever will be our country's most powerful resource in peace or in war."

Springfield Union News Daily, June 15th, 1954

by Lincoln's iconic address. It gained momentum when the Knights of Columbus adopted it, sparking a push for its official integration. The campaign reached a turning point with a sermon by George M. Docherty, which President Eisenhower attended, linking the pledge to America's unique values and divine belief.

In 1954, moved by Docherty's words, Eisenhower urged Congress to amend the pledge, resulting in the formal inclusion of "under God." This not only reinforced the nation's collective faith but also served as a symbolic counter to communist principles. The revised Pledge of Allegiance thus became a declaration of the American ethos, infusing the nation's religious conviction into its patriotic expression.

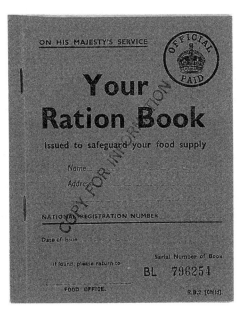

Sample Child's Ration Book

Britain Celebrates: Farewell to 14-Year Ration Era - July 4th

For over a decade after World War II, Britain endured a strict rationing system, a necessary response to the wartime blockades that severely limited imports. This system, which affected everything from food to fuel, aimed to ensure fair distribution and prioritize essential services, including the military. The British populace, used to managing with less, had to contend with rations even for basics like bacon and petrol, with the system occasionally tightening its grip in response to events like the disastrous rains of 1946.

The continued rationing post-war became a source of public frustration and a political hot potato, with the Conservative Party leveraging it to win the 1951 elections on promises of easing restrictions. Gradually, the government

One person's weekly rationing allowance in England in 1951

lifted the rationing, with petrol in 1950 and sweets in 1953, culminating in the end of food rationing, which had persisted for 14 years.

The final lifting of food rationing was met with widespread relief and celebration, signifying a return to normalcy. Though the rationing era had imposed a uniformity on products, particularly affecting the variety in the cheese industry, it also showcased the resilience and adaptability of the British people. The cessation of rationing not only brought about immediate changes but also left a lasting influence on the nation's cultural and political landscape, encapsulating an unforgettable period in Britain's post-war history.

Algeria on the Move: Seeking Freedom from France - November 1st

The Algerian War of Independence (1954-1962) stands as a crucial chapter in the decolonization narrative, ending with Algeria's sovereignty after a prolonged struggle against French colonial rule. Tracing its roots to France's 1830 invasion, Algeria was fully integrated into France by 1834, but restrictive policies like the Indigenous Code

The Algerian Revolution

limited Muslims' rights, sparking nationalist fervor post-World War II. Ferhat Abbas and other leaders' push for autonomy, illustrated in the 1943 Algerian People's Manifesto, eventually shifted towards militancy with the formation of the FLN and its armed wing in 1954. The conflict transcended a mere fight for independence, involving deep-seated internal conflicts and harsh French countermeasures that eroded international support.

The 1960s saw a turn towards Algerian independence, underscored by significant demonstrations and a UN resolution that led to the 1962 Évian Accords. However, the transition was marred by assassination attempts on President Charles de Gaulle, military insurgencies, and resistance from factions like the OAS.

This era, characterized by extensive casualties, acts of war, and the displacement of European-Algerians, symbolizes the intense and unwavering quest for national self-rule.

Political Events

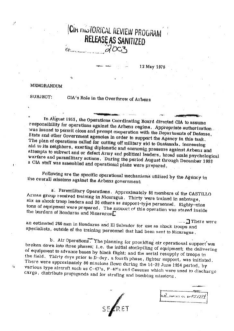

Internal CIA memo describing its role in the Coup

Guatemala Shift: Armas Leads After CIA Coup - June 27th

Guatemala witnessed a dramatic power shift when a CIA operation, code-named PBSuccess, deposed its democratically elected President, Jacobo Árbenz. This move terminated the Guatemalan Revolution and initiated a series of U.S.-backed authoritarian regimes.

The revolution began in 1944 with a public uprising against dictator Jorge Ubico. Juan José Arévalo, elected in the first democratic poll, laid the democracy's groundwork. His successor, Árbenz, introduced land reforms benefiting peasants but displeased the U.S., already combating communism in the Cold War era. Further fueling U.S. concerns was lobbying from the United Fruit Company (UFC), which felt threatened by these reforms.

In response, President Dwight D. Eisenhower, who had UFC-connected advisors, adopted an anti-communist stance. By August 1953, the CIA

Carlos Castillo Armas

launched PBSuccess, arming a 480-strong force led by Carlos Castillo Armas. Despite initial setbacks, psychological warfare and the fear of U.S. intervention broke the Guatemalan Army's resolve, leading to Árbenz's resignation and Armas' subsequent rise to power.

This coup drew global criticism, triggered lasting anti-U.S. sentiments in Latin America, and led to a dark era for Guatemala, marked by dictatorship, civil wars, and human rights atrocities.

J. Ernest Wilkins Sr.

Wilkins Breaks Barriers: First Black Man in U.S. Cabinet Meeting - July 2nd

Jesse Ernest Wilkins Sr. stands as a central figure in American history, being the first African American to serve in a sub-cabinet position and attend White House cabinet meetings. Appointed by President Eisenhower as Undersecretary of Labor for International Labor Affairs in 1954, Wilkins was also a member of influential committees such as the Equality Committee. His tenure was not without strife; he faced attempts to be sidelined by Secretary of Labor James P. Mitchell, resulting in health and career struggles.

Wilkins's commitment to civil rights was unwavering. While with the Civil Rights Commission, he experienced firsthand discrimination in Montgomery, Alabama, but persevered, continuing his work from Maxwell Air Force Base. His leadership extended to the Methodist Church, where he became the first African American on the Judicial Council and later its president. He also served as the Grand Polemarch of Kappa Alpha Psi Fraternity, Inc. Despite the challenges, Wilkins's death shortly after resigning did not diminish his lasting impact as a barrier-breaking leader dedicated to civil rights and equality.

Bilderberg's First: Elite Summit in Netherlands - May 29th-31st

The Bilderberg Meeting, initiated in the mid-1950s, represents an exclusive annual summit aimed at fostering Euro-American relations. Its founding objective was to prevent global conflict, but it has since pivoted to bolstering free-market capitalism. The conference unites influential figures from

Bilderberg Hotel in the Netherlands

politics, business, finance, and academia, who engage in off-the-record discussions to shape global policy while maintaining confidentiality, fueling widespread conspiracy theories.

Named after its first venue, the Hotel de Bilderberg in the Netherlands, the forum was intended to address increasing anti-American sentiment in Western Europe. Notables like Prince Bernhard of the Netherlands were instrumental in its establishment, which initially included 50 European and 11 American delegates.

From its successful inception, the meeting became an annual fixture, hosted across various countries and gradually extending its scope beyond transatlantic cooperation to broader capitalist principles. The group's secretive nature occasionally breaks surface, drawing public attention and debate, most notably during their public endorsement of a European Council President. This blend of privacy and occasional public visibility continues to shroud the Bilderberg Meeting with a veil of mystery.

Senate Rebuffs McCarthy: Dishonor Called Out - December 2nd

Sen. McCarthy at The Army–McCarthy hearings

In 1954, the U.S. Senate decisively censured Senator Joseph McCarthy, culminating a national saga of anti-communist fervor. The controversial senator had been at the forefront of communist hunts, which led to televised hearings against the U.S. Army. Accusations flew between McCarthy and the Army regarding alleged preferential treatment for an associate of McCarthy's, amidst claims of communist infiltration. The hearings, broadcast by major networks, staged dramatic exchanges, notably between McCarthy and Joseph Welch, the Army's counsel. Welch's poignant challenge to McCarthy's decency became emblematic of the senator's declining influence. When Welch denounced McCarthy for attacking a young lawyer in his firm over supposed communist ties, the nation witnessed the unraveling of McCarthy's reign of fear.

The Senate's censure by a decisive vote indicated McCarthy's waning power. Fred Fisher, despite McCarthy's attempts to tarnish him, later soared in his legal career, joining the elite ranks at the Hale & Dorr law firm. As for McCarthy, his voice dwindled to empty Senate chambers and he succumbed to alcoholism, passing away at just 48 in 1957.

Other Notable Events

Bannister's Record: Mile in Under 4 Minutes - May 6th

Roger Bannister, an English neurologist and middle-distance runner, made athletic history not by winning Olympic medals but by breaking the seemingly insurmountable four-minute barrier for the mile run. In an era

where the record had been narrowly unattainable for years, Bannister's quest culminated at Oxford's Iffley Road track. Despite challenging weather conditions and a demanding day job as a junior doctor,

Roger Bannister Breaks the 4-minute Mile

he seized the opportunity when the winds calmed. With fellow athletes Chris Chataway and Chris Brasher setting the pace, Bannister finished with a record-setting time of 3 minutes and 59.4 seconds. His record was a monumental achievement that transcended sports, influencing both athletics and academic medicine. Bannister's feat became a symbol of human potential, a beacon of possibility in post-war Britain, and his legacy, fortified by his later medical career, remains an enduring inspiration.

Lake Ontario's New Hero: Marilyn Bell Conquers - September 9th

Support for the brave swimmer

Marilyn Bell Di Lascio, a determined Canadian teenager, became a national sensation when she accomplished the unprecedented feat of swimming across Lake Ontario. She embarked on this daring journey not for fame or fortune but as a patriotic challenge, spurred on by the exclusion of Canadian swimmers from a sponsored event. Starting alongside Florence Chadwick, the renowned American swimmer, Bell persevered through treacherous waters that thwarted Chadwick's efforts.

Bell's swim was fraught with obstacles: she battled high waves, frigid temperatures, and even lamprey eels. Yet, sustained by a mix of Pablum, corn syrup, and lemon juice, and driven by the unwavering support of her crew, she swam for nearly 21 hours, covering a distance much greater than the planned 32 miles due to harsh winds and primitive navigation. Her arrival was met by a massive crowd, and she was greeted as a hero, showered with gifts and accolades, and even received the originally promised prize. Her remarkable triumph was a testament to resilience and became a celebrated moment in Canadian sports history.

Evelyn Margaret Ay, 1954 Miss America

Miss America's TV Debut: Pageantry Goes Prime Time - September 11th

The Miss America pageant, a long-standing symbol of grace and beauty, took a significant leap into the future as it was broadcast on television for the first time. This historic event brought the excitement of the competition from the Boardwalk Hall in Atlantic City directly into homes across the nation. Viewers were enraptured as Evelyn Margaret Ay, Miss Pennsylvania, was crowned Miss America, marking a notable first for her state in receiving this honor.

The pageant, judged by luminaries including the soon-to-be princess Grace Kelly, not only celebrated beauty but also became a launchpad for success. Miriam Stevenson, a Top 10 finisher, went on to win Miss USA and Miss Universe titles, while Carlene King Johnson, although not winning at Miss America as Miss Vermont, claimed the Miss USA crown the following year. The broadcast captivated a record-breaking 27 million Americans, establishing Miss America as a beloved national tradition and a pinnacle of television entertainment, consistently drawing massive audiences every year since its television inception.

Hemingway's Triumph: Nobel Literature Prize in Hand - October 28th

Ernest Hemingway Receiving his 1954 Nobel Prize for Literature

Ernest Hemingway, a literary titan known for his concise and impactful prose, was awarded the Nobel Prize in Literature. Celebrated for his influence on 20th-century fiction, Hemingway's narrative mastery shines in "The Old Man and the Sea," a work that played a significant role in the Swedish Academy's decision.

His storytelling, marked by themes of love, war, loss, and the rawness of the human experience, culminated in this recognition, making him the fifth American laureate. Hemingway's novel, "The Old Man and the Sea," is a poignant tale of a Cuban fisherman's harrowing sea adventure, reflecting his own fishing experiences. This short yet profound narrative not only earned him the Nobel Prize but also the Pulitzer Prize for Fiction, solidifying his status as a defining voice in modern literature. Hemingway's contributions have left an indelible mark on the literary world, resonating through his exploration of life's profound complexities.

Sporting News Redefined: 'Sports Illustrated' Launches - August 16th

"Sports Illustrated," a name now synonymous with sports journalism, made its grand entrance, offering vivid color photography and in-depth sports reporting. The magazine, poised to become an icon, was an innovative force from the start, setting the bar high with features like scouting reports that enhanced televised games and monthly awards for high school football players.

Although initially focusing on the leisure sports of the elite, under Andre Laguerre's editorial leadership, it shifted towards the rising national interest in professional football and other mainstream sports. Laguerre's vision was crucial in expanding the magazine's popularity, doubling its circulation, and pioneering the "bonus piece" – a long-form end-of-issue article. His most famous contribution, the annual Swimsuit Issue, remains a cultural phenomenon.

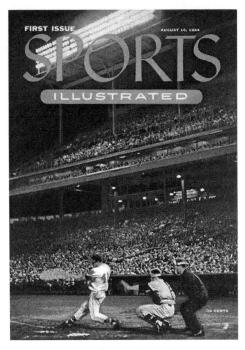

Sports Illustrated, 1st Issue

Sports Illustrated's legacy of journalistic excellence, seen in its trailblazing use of color photos and detailed sports coverage by eminent writers, has endured through the decades, solidifying its place as a cornerstone of sports media.

Chapter II: Crime & Punishment 1954

Major Crime Events

Patterson's End: Phenix City's Dark Tale Begins - June 18th

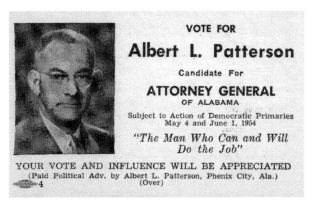

VOTE FOR

Albert L. Patterson

Candidate For

ATTORNEY GENERAL
OF ALABAMA

Subject to Action of Democratic Primaries
May 4 and June 1, 1954

*"The Man Who Can and Will
Do the Job"*

YOUR VOTE AND INFLUENCE WILL BE APPRECIATED
(Paid Political Adv. by Albert L. Patterson, Phenix City, Ala.)
4   (Over)

A 1954 Albert Patterson for Attorney General palm card

In Phenix City, Alabama, the murder of Albert Patterson, who had just secured the Democratic nomination for Attorney General, marked a shocking escalation in the fight against corruption. His assassination led to a swift response from Governor Gordon Persons, who declared martial law and sent in the National Guard. The legal system, previously tainted by collusion with local crime, was overhauled as special prosecutors stepped in, leading to a massive purge of the city's criminal rings with over 700 indictments. Albert Fuller faced conviction for Patterson's murder, and in the wake of his father's death, John Malcolm Patterson took the reins as Attorney General, later rising to Governor, relentlessly pursuing his father's anti-crime agenda. This tragic event triggered a significant cleanup of Alabama's political landscape, with Patterson's legacy becoming a symbol of the state's commitment to law and order.

U.S. Capitol Attack: Puerto Rican Nationalists Fire - March 1st

In a daring act of political protest, four Puerto Rican nationalists opened fire on the U.S. House of Representatives chamber, wounding five congressmen. Their aim: to draw attention to the cause of Puerto Rico's independence.

The attack, led by Lolita Lebrón, was meticulously planned, beginning in Manhattan and culminating in the halls of the U.S. Capitol. As they unleashed gunfire, Lebrón's cry for a free Puerto Rico echoed through the chamber.

"Guard Congress After Gunfire," Boston Daily Globe

The group was promptly apprehended, leading to further crackdowns, including the arrest of Puerto Rican Nationalist Party leader Pedro Albizu Campos, though he was not directly implicated in the attack. The repercussions for Campos were harsh, with legal and health troubles plaguing his later years. This incident marked a dramatic moment in the struggle for Puerto Rican sovereignty, leaving a complex legacy of political fervor and violent resistance.

Sam Sheppard Mugshot

Sheppard Mystery: Brutal Murder Sparks Notorious Trial - July 4th

Dr. Samuel Sheppard was immersed in media uproar following his wife Marilyn's murder. Local Cleveland papers, especially Cleveland Press, insinuated a family plot to shield him. In this media-heavy environment, he was controversially convicted of murder.

Initial appeals failed, but F. Lee Bailey later secured a U.S. Supreme Court ruling which highlighted trial injustices, including media influence and a biased judge.

In a 1966 retrial, Bailey skillfully challenged prosecution claims, emphasizing evidence suggesting a left-handed murderer, whereas Sheppard was right-handed. After deliberation, the jury acquitted Sheppard, elevating Bailey's legal stature.

Sam Sheppard's Wife and Son

Years later, in a heartfelt quest for truth and redemption, his determined son initiated crucial DNA testing on his father's exhumed remains. These 1997 tests provided a bittersweet exoneration for Sheppard.

Their intertwined fates sealed, both Dr. Sheppard and Marilyn's ashes were solemnly laid to rest together in a mausoleum at Knollwood Cemetery, Mayfield Heights, Ohio. The tale serves as a powerful testament to the complex interplay of media, justice, and truth.

Veterans' Controversy: Land Board Scandal Erupts – November

In 1954, Texas was gripped by the Veterans Land Board Scandal. Stemming from the 1946 Veterans Land Act, Texas Legislature set up a $25 million bond to purchase land for World War II veterans, a figure which grew to $100 million by 1951. The intention: veterans could buy the land at 3% interest over 40 years, with the stipulation that each loan was under $7,500 and the plots were at least 20 acres.

Commissioner J. Bascom Giles

Texas Veterans Land Board Brochure, 1946

The scandal erupted when journalist Ken Towery exposed a scheme. Businessmen were tricking mostly illiterate Hispanic and African American veterans into unknowingly signing land grant applications, pocketing the money meant for them. These veterans were largely oblivious to the transactions. Some even believed they were receiving land as a veteran entitlement or compensation.

Texas Veterans Land Board chairman, Bascom Giles, attempted to shift blame, raising more suspicions. Investigations unveiled widespread fraud in several counties. The repercussions were severe: Giles was imprisoned, hefty fines were imposed, and the integrity of prominent figures like Governor Allan Shivers was questioned. Towery's exposé earned him a 1955 Pulitzer Prize.

Chapter III: Entertainment 1954

Silver Screen

Top Film of 1954: White Christmas

"White Christmas", a musical romance directed by Michael Curtiz, debuted in 1954, starring Bing Crosby as Captain Bob Wallace and Danny Kaye as Private Phil Davis. As two WWII veterans turned performers, they collaborate with two singing sisters, striving to save the Vermont inn of their former General from financial turmoil. This film reintroduced the iconic "White Christmas" song, originally from the 1942 Holiday Inn, amid other Irving Berlin classics.

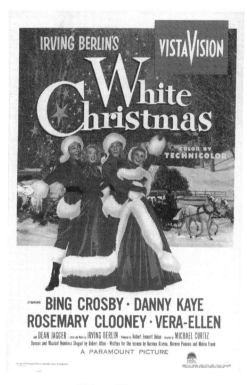

White Christmas

Despite pioneering the widescreen process, VistaVision, the film's appeal transcended technological feats, grossing $30 million domestically, and becoming 1954's highest-grossing film. Critics provided a medley of opinions; some appreciated its visual charm and all-star cast, while others desired deeper substance. Today, it's heralded as a classic, exuding the festive spirit of Christmas and the enchantment of its era's musicals.

The film's enduring charm inspired a stage adaptation, Irving Berlin's White Christmas, which premiered in San Francisco in 2004. This musical adaptation toured cities including Boston, Buffalo, and Los Angeles, even gracing Broadway's Marquis Theatre in 2008. The UK witnessed its magic from 2006 to 2008, with significant runs in Manchester, Sunderland, and an eventual climax in London's West End in 2014. This continuous adaptation, bridging the screen to the stage, accentuates the timeless allure of White Christmas in the world of entertainment.

Remaining Top 3

20,000 Leagues Under the Sea

20,000 Leagues Under the Sea

A 1954 cinematic endeavor directed by Richard Fleischer, springs from the imaginative depths of Jules Verne's 1870 novel. This Walt Disney personally produced spectacle, distributed by Buena Vista, showcases the talents of Kirk Douglas, James Mason, Paul Lukas, and Peter Lorre, all framed in the groundbreaking CinemaScope and vibrant Technicolor. As one of Disney's initial ventures into feature-length productions, the film became iconic for its captivating battle against a giant squid and Mason's magnetic portrayal of Captain Nemo. Garnering two Oscars for its art direction and special effects, it is recognized as a precursor to steampunk. While critics like Bosley Crowther of The New York Times found it captivating, particularly for younger audiences, its faithfulness to Verne's novel is both celebrated and critiqued. Certain deviations, like the atomic-powered submarine rather than the original's battery-powered one, offer a fresh cinematic perspective. Current critiques maintain its significance, with a 90% approval on Rotten Tomatoes, highlighting its enduring charm and meticulous adaptation.

Demetrius and the Gladiators

Demetrius and the Gladiators

The 1954 biblical drama film from 20th Century Fox, serves as the sequel to "The Robe." Directed by Delmer Daves and penned by Philip Dunne, it delves into the life of Demetrius, portrayed by Victor Mature. As a Christian slave, he grapples with his beliefs and the brutal world of gladiatorial combat in the Roman Coliseum. Susan Hayward shines as Messalina, wife to Claudius and counterpart to the unhinged Emperor Caligula, played by Jay Robinson. The tale spirals from faith to betrayal, with Demetrius's love, Lucia, seemingly meeting a tragic end, pushing him towards vengeance and a departure from his Christian values. Yet redemption awaits as truths unravel, leading to political upheavals and a newfound hope for Christians in Rome. The film, dressed in CinemaScope and Technicolor, was a massive commercial success, grossing $26 million in North America. Critically, its mix of spectacle, romance, and drama earned accolades, with many deeming it superior in entertainment to its predecessor.

 Top 1954 Movies at The Domestic Box Office (the-numbers.com)

Rank	Title	Release Date	1954 Gross
1	White Christmas	Apr 27, 1954	$30,000,000
2	20,000 Leagues Under the Sea	Dec 23, 1954	$28,200,000

Rank	Title	Release Date	1954 Gross
3	Demetrius and the Gladiators	Jun 18, 1954	$26,000,000
4	Rear Window	Sep 1, 1954	$22,953,835
5	The Caine Mutiny	Jun 24, 1954	$21,800,000
6	Gone with the Wind	Dec 15, 1939	$16,666,667
7	The Egyptian	Aug 24, 1954	$15,000,000
8	The High and the Mighty	Jul 3, 1954	$10,400,000
9	On the Waterfront	Jul 28, 1954	$9,600,000
10	Desiree	Nov 17, 1954	$9,000,000

Other Film Releases

Johnny Guitar

1954 was a pivotal year in cinema. The golden age of Hollywood, the peak of Italian Neo-realism, and the post-war blossoming of Japanese film converged to produce an abundance of cinematic gems. Among these, six films stood out for their later cult followings, despite not initially dominating the box office: "Johnny Guitar," "Sansho the Bailiff," "La Strada," "The Caine Mutiny," "Journey to Italy," and "A Star Is Born."

"Johnny Guitar," directed by Nicholas Ray, was more than just a western. It carried undertones of the McCarthy era, creating

Sansho the Bailiff

La Strada

layers of subtext about persecution and conformity. Joan Crawford's outstanding performance as Vienna, a saloon owner, stood out, challenging the traditional roles of women in westerns. Over time, its thematic depth has attracted directors and film enthusiasts alike, with legends like Martin Scorsese and François Truffaut expressing their admiration.

Kenji Mizoguchi's "Sansho the Bailiff" is a heart-wrenching tale of feudal Japan. It delves into the struggles of two aristocratic children who are separated from their family and sold into slavery. Mizoguchi's exquisite craftsmanship, combined with the film's profound exploration of human endurance, has made it a staple in film studies across the world.

"La Strada" represents the genius of Federico Fellini. The film, focusing on a young girl's adventures with a traveling circus and her complex relationship with a strongman, is a showcase of Fellini's unparalleled ability to weave reality with dream-like sequences. It played a foundational role in establishing

Italian cinema's reputation on the global stage.

The Caine Mutiny

"The Caine Mutiny," set during the tumultuous backdrop of World War II, offers a compelling tale of naval discipline, moral dilemmas, and human conflict. With Humphrey Bogart leading the cast, the film's portrayal of the strain of leadership and the complexities of duty has resonated with audiences for decades.

Roberto Rossellini's "Journey to Italy" is more than just a travelogue. It's an exploration of marriage and emotional disconnect set against the evocative landscapes of Naples. The intimate portrayal of the couple, played by George

Journey to Italy

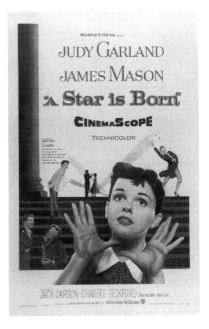

A Star Is Born

Sanders and Ingrid Bergman, combined with Rossellini's observational style, makes it an early precursor to the character-driven narratives of modern cinema.

Concluding this list is "A Star Is Born," a tale of love, ambition, and the pitfalls of fame. Judy Garland's mesmerizing performance, combined with the film's candid portrayal of the entertainment industry, has led many to regard this iteration as the most impactful among its various remakes.

In sum, 1954 saw the release of numerous films, but these six distinguished themselves by pushing boundaries and exploring new thematic terrains. Their enduring popularity, critical acclaim in subsequent years, and passionate fanbase attest to their rightful place as some of the year's most influential cult movies.

The 11th Golden Globe Awards – Friday, January 22nd, 1954

Best Motion Picture – Drama:
The Robe

Best Performance in a Motion Picture
Drama – Actor:
Spencer Tracy (The Actress)

Best Performance in a Motion Picture
Drama – Actress:
Audrey Hepburn (Roman Holiday)

Best Performance in a Motion Picture –
Comedy or Musical – Actor:
David Niven (The Moon Is Blue)

Best Performance in a Motion Picture –
Comedy or Musical - Actress:
Ethel Merman (Call Me Madam)

Best Supporting Performance in a Motion
Picture – Actor:
Frank Sinatra (From Here to Eternity)

Best Supporting Performance in a Motion
Picture – Actress:
Grace Kelly (Mogambo)

Best Director:
Fred Zinnemann (From Here to Eternity)

Best Screenplay:
Helen Deutsch (Lili)

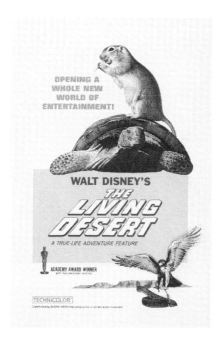

Special Achievement Award:
Walt Disney (The Living Desert)

7th British Academy Film Awards – 1954

These categories didn't exist in 1954: Best Direction, Best Supporting Actor, Best Supporting Actress, and Best Screenplay.

Best Film: Forbidden Games

Best British Film: Genevieve

Best Foreign Actor:
Marlon Brando (Julius Caesar)

Best Foreign Actress:
Leslie Caron (Lili)

Best British Actor:
John Gielgud (Julius Caesar)

Best British Actress:
Audrey Hepburn (Roman Holiday)

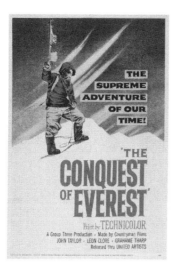

Best Documentary:
The Conquest of Everest

The 26th Academy Awards – Thursday, March 25th, 1954 - Simultaneously at the RKO Pantages Theatre in Hollywood and the NBC Center Theatre in New York City

♉ Winners

Best Actor in a Leading Role:
William Holden (Stalag 17)

Best Actress in a Leading Role:
Audrey Hepburn (Roman Holiday)

Best Supporting Actor:
Frank Sinatra (From Here to Eternity)

Best Supporting Actress:
Donna Reed (From Here to Eternity)

Best Director:
Fred Zinnemann (From Here to Eternity)

Best Cinematography (Black-and-White):
Burnett Guffey (From Here to Eternity)

Best Cinematography (Color):
Loyal Griggs (Shane)

Best Film:
From Here to Eternity

Top of the Charts

The 1950s were a transformative period in the music world, marking the bridge between the sentimental ballads of the 1940s and the revolutionary sounds of the 1960s. As post-war optimism spread, the 50s saw the birth of rock 'n' roll, capturing the hearts of the younger generation. Icons like Elvis Presley burst onto the scene, bringing with them an electrifying energy and swagger. Concurrently, the soothing melodies of crooners and balladeers provided a comforting backdrop. The rise of doo-wop emphasized harmony and rhythm, while the roots of Motown began to take shape, setting the stage for a musical revolution. Throughout the decade, the jukebox became a staple in local diners, echoing the chart-toppers of this dynamic era.

The Student Prince

Top Album: "The Student Prince" by Mario Lanza

Mario Lanza's "The Student Prince," quickly became a definitive sound of the 1950s. The album, drawing from the beloved operetta by Sigmund Romberg and Dorothy Donnelly, showcased Lanza's extraordinary vocal talent to the broader public. Although Lanza was ousted from the MGM film over conflicts, his voice persisted on the soundtrack, with "Serenade" and "Drink, Drink, Drink" becoming quintessential anthems of his passionate tenor. The album's seamless blend of operatic richness and widespread appeal not only brought it immense popularity but also solidified Lanza's legacy as a quintessential voice of his era. "The Student Prince" stands out as a memorable triumph in Lanza's distinguished discography, continuing to be revered as a testament to his enduring influence in the world of music.

Best Albums and Singles

In 1954, the music world pulsated with diverse sonorous tones. Jazz enthusiasts reveled in the innovative rhythms of Miles Davis' "Birth Of The Cool" and the energy of Art Blakey's two "Night At Birdland" volumes.

Birth Of The Cool

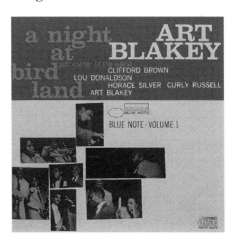

Night At Birdland

Chet Baker brought intimacy with "Chet Baker Sings" while Billie Holiday's emotive "Lady Sings The Blues" resonated with many.

Chet Baker Sings

Lady Sings The Blues

On the pop front, Frank Sinatra serenaded listeners with "Songs for Young Lovers," while Jackie Gleason set the mood with "Music, Martinis, & Memories."

Songs for Young Lovers   Music, Martinis, & Memories

Not to be outdone, the singles chart was ablaze with Doris Day's heartwarming "Secret Love" and The Chordettes' whimsical "Mister Sandman."

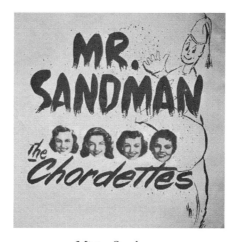

Secret Love   Mister Sandman

The Crew-Cuts introduced everyone to the infectious "Sh-Boom," and Eddie Fisher's velvety voice graced the airwaves twice.

Sh-Boom

Indeed, 1954 was a year where melodies nostalgically danced in the hearts of listeners.

🎵 Top Albums 1954 (tsort.info):

1. Mario Lanza - The Student Prince
2. Miles Davis - Birth Of The Cool
3. Art Blakey - A Night At Birdland, Vol 1
4. Chet Baker - Chet Baker Sings
5. Jackie Gleason - Music, Martinis, & Memories
6. Louis Armstrong - Louis Armstrong Plays WC Handy
7. Billie Holiday - Lady Sings The Blues
8. Clifford Brown & Max Roach - Clifford Brown & Max Roach
9. Frank Sinatra - Songs for Young Lovers
10. Art Blakey - A Night At Birdland, Vol 2
11. June Christy - Something Cool
12. Max Steiner - Gone with the Wind

🎵 Top Singles 1954 (tsort.info):

1. Doris Day - Secret Love
2. The Chordettes - Mister Sandman

3. The Crew-Cuts - Sh-Boom (Life Could Be a Dream)
4. Kitty Kallen - Little Things Mean a Lot
5. Rosemary Clooney - Hey There
6. Tony Bennett - Stranger in Paradise
7. Eddie Fisher - I Need You Now
8. Perry Como - Wanted
9. Don Cornell - Hold My Hand
10. Eddie Fisher - Oh My Papa (O Mein Papa)
11. Four Aces - Three Coins in the Fountain
12. Rosemary Clooney - This Ole House

 Award Winners

Neither the Grammy Awards nor the Brit Awards existed in 1954.

Television

In 1954, the world of television was a dazzling spectacle of innovation and imagination. While America basked in the warmth of 'Father Knows Best' and cheered for 'Lassie', Britain, with its singular and influential BBC channel, showcased the wit of 'Zoo Quest' and the timeless insights of 'Panorama'. Despite broadcasting limitations, such as the endearing "Toddler's Truce", the era thrived on creativity. The UK's television landscape, although limited, became a cultural touchstone, setting precedents for decades. The programming of 1954 wasn't merely for leisure; it reflected the era's

Father Knows Best

zeitgeist, influenced public opinion, and established legacies that resonate even today.

Lassie

Zoo Quest

Panorama

Roses Parade in Color: Coast-to-Coast TV First - January 1st

An aerial view of a Tournament of Roses parade

In 1954, a mesmerizing burst of colors danced across American screens, enchanting viewers nationwide. The venerable Rose Parade, a cherished tradition since 1890, became a vibrant tapestry of tones as color television made its monumental debut. Through the combined wizardry of RCA, NBC, and F. W. Woolworth Co., this New Year's spectacle was the first to shine in the NTSC color format. It wasn't just a parade; it was a moment where history, technology, and magic intertwined, forever elevating the television experience.

FCC Greenlights Color TV: New Broadcasting Era - January 22nd

The television world was painted in a fresh spectrum of possibilities when the Federal Communications Commission (FCC) embraced the future by

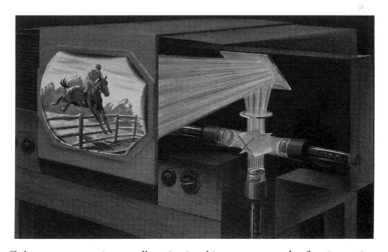

Color converter using small projection kinetoscopes and refractive optics

approving the RCA Dot Sequential Color System, a brainchild birthed by RCA in 1949. This landmark decision signified the dawn of a new broadcasting era, propelling TV from monochromatic memories into vibrant vistas. The canvas of entertainment was forever transformed, ushering in a richer, more dynamic viewing experience for audiences everywhere.

Steve Allen Launches "Tonight": Late-Night TV Begins - September 27th

Steve Allen on the The Tonight Show set

On a historic evening in 1954, Steve Allen didn't just kick off "Tonight", he literally wrote the rulebook for late-night TV shenanigans. With zesty monologues, cheeky audience banter, and even some outdoor mischief, Allen's blueprint became the golden standard. Sure, pioneers like Jerry Lester were in the game earlier, but it was Allen's mix of comedy sketches, melodies, and chats that made "Tonight" more than just a fleeting moment; it became a cornerstone in TV's nightly lineup. And as legends from Carson to Fallon took the baton, each sprinkled their magic, ensuring "Tonight" forever twinkles in the television galaxy.

"Father Knows Best" Hits TV: Radio Star's New Home - October 3rd

"Father Knows Best" transitioned from radio waves to the TV screen, capturing hearts once again. The sitcom, centered on the Andersons from Springfield, was a delightful peek into mid-century, middle-class America. While radio's Jim Anderson was a tad more sarcastic, demanding chuckles, TV brought a softer, more relatable family dynamic. Robert Young's

Father Knows Best

portrayal of Jim shifted from a sharp-tongued patriarch to a warm-hearted dad, harmonizing with the series' tonal shift. The show, with its delightful escapades and heartfelt moments, immortalized the Andersons as TV's quintessential family.

BBC's '1984': Orwell Adaptation Stirs Debate - December 12th

BBC's adaptation of George Orwell's "1984" ignited a firestorm of controversy, as viewers were confronted with Orwell's chilling vision of a totalitarian regime. The production was overshadowed by accusations of subversiveness, and the intense content stirred public outcry so much that it provoked debate in Parliament. While some criticized its portrayal as horrifying and potentially disruptive, others hailed the bold presentation, noting that some depicted inhuman practices were already realities under certain regimes. As polarizing views swirled, the British Broadcasting Corporation stood firm, offering viewers a stark window into a dystopian world and sparking nationwide reflection on freedom and control.

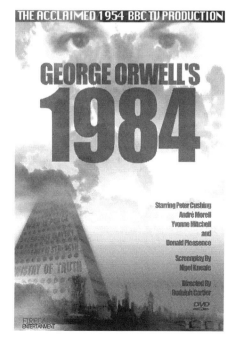

THE ACCLAIMED 1954 BBC TV PRODUCTION

GEORGE ORWELL'S

1984

Starring Peter Cushing
André Morell
Yvonne Mitchell
and
Donald Pleasence

Screenplay By
Nigel Kneale

Directed By
Rudolph Cartier

1984

📺 Television Ratings 1954 (classic-tv.com)

1953-54 Shows

Rank	Show	Estimated Audience
1.	I Love Lucy	15,288,000
2.	Dragnet	13,832,000
3.	Arthur Godfrey's Talent Scouts	11,336,000
4.	You Bet Your Life	11,336,000
5.	The Milton Berle Show	10,452,000
6.	Arthur Godfrey and His Friends	10,114,000
7.	Ford Theatre	10,088,000
8.	The Jackie Gleason Show	9,906,000
9.	Fireside Theatre	9,464,000
10.	The Colgate Comedy Hour	9,412,000

1954-55 Shows

Rank	Show	Estimated Audience
1.	I Love Lucy	15,135,100
2.	The Jackie Gleason Show	13,016,800
3.	Dragnet	12,924,700
4.	You Bet Your Life	12,587,000
5.	The Toast of the Town	12,157,200
6.	Disneyland	12,003,700

7.	The Jack Benny Show	11,758,100
8.	The George Gobel Show	10,806,400
9.	Ford Theatre	10,714,300
10.	December Bride	10,652,900

♛ Award Winners In 1954

Both the Golden Globe Awards and B.A.F.T.A. Awards only recognized films (the latter was called the British Academy Film Awards in this year).

The 5th Primetime Emmy Awards - Thursday, February 11th, 1954 - Hollywood Palladium in Los Angeles, California

Best Situation Comedy:
I Love Lucy

Best Dramatic Program:
The United States Steel Hour

Best Actor:
Donald O'Connor

Best Actress:
Eve Arden

Best Supporting Actor:
Art Carney

Best Supporting Actress:
Vivian Vance

Best Audience Participation, Quiz or Panel
Program: This Is Your Life

Best Mystery, Action or Adventure
Program: Dragnet

Best Variety Program:
Omnibus

Chapter IV: Sports Review 1954

American Sports

Lakers Dunk NBA Championship - April 12th

The NBA Champion, Minneapolis Lakers

In the tightly contested NBA World Championship Series, the Minneapolis Lakers secured their championship title, marking their fifth win in a span of seven years since 1949. Facing off against the formidable Syracuse Nationals, the Lakers represented the Western Division with confidence. The competition was fierce, as the Lakers started strong with an initial victory, only to see the teams alternate wins thereafter. Yet, in the end, the Lakers demonstrated their prowess, sealing their triumph with a seven-point lead on home ground. This thrilling series was condensed into a mere thirteen days, with both teams showing stamina and skill, playing 13 games throughout the 28-day postseason.

Doris Hart

Doris Hart: Tennis Queen of the US Championship - September 6th

In a thrilling finale at the U.S. National Championships, Doris Hart emerged as the undeniable tennis queen. Second-seeded Hart showcased sheer resilience against Louise Brough, winning with a scoreline of 6–8, 6–1, 8–6. With this victory, she added another feather to her cap, completing the career grand slam in singles. The contest was even more enthralling considering the absence of three-time defending champion, Maureen Connolly, sidelined due to a horse-riding accident. Amidst strong competition, with eight seeded players including the likes of Beverly Baker Fleitz and Margaret Osborne duPont, Hart's championship win left a significant mark in tennis history.

Red Wings Soar to Stanley Cup Victory - April 16th

The Detroit Red Wings team celebrating their victory

In the gripping Stanley Cup Finals, the Detroit Red Wings battled against the defending champions, Montreal Canadiens, marking their fourth consecutive showdown in the Finals. Detroit sealed a 4-3 series win, marking their sixth Stanley Cup victory overall. The path to this monumental clash saw Montreal besting the Boston Bruins 4-0, while Detroit outplayed the Toronto Maple Leafs with a 4-1 series win. The series reached an electrifying climax when Tony Leswick's overtime shot in the seventh game, which took a bizarre deflection off Montreal's Doug Harvey's glove, found its way into the net. The victory was made all the more remarkable as the Canadiens, stunned by the unexpected goal, left the ice without the traditional handshake.

Giants Crush Indians: World Series Champs - October 2nd

The New York Giants, World Series winner

The World Series saw the New York Giants clinch a stunning victory, sweeping the Cleveland Indians, a team that had an impressive AL-record 111 wins that season. This series featured iconic moments, such as "The Catch" by Willie Mays and Dusty Rhodes' game-sealing hit in Game 1. The Giants' manager, Leo Durocher, achieved his only World Series win. This match-up presented notable finalities: the last World Series games at both the Polo Grounds and Cleveland Stadium. Simultaneously, a scheduled NFL game was postponed, setting the stage for a memorable NFL championship clash. In a rare twist, this was the first World Series since 1948 without the Yankees.

British Sports

Wolves Conquer: English Football League Champs - April 24th

In the 1953–54 season, the Wolverhampton Wanderers, fondly known as the Wolves, achieved a historic first by conquering the First Division League championship, the pinnacle of English football at the time. Battling it out

The Wolverhampton Wanderers

among 22 top-tier teams, Wolves not only made a monumental mark but also managed to surpass their local adversaries, West Bromwich Albion. The triumph was especially sweet for the Wolves, as they had previously come excitingly close, finishing as runners-up on three separate occasions. The league format saw each team play the other twice, with victories earning two points, draws one, and defeats none.

Connolly Conquers: Wimbledon's Women's Singles Champion - July 3rd

In the grand lawns of the Wimbledon Championships, Maureen Connolly displayed remarkable ability, emerging as the Women's Singles Champion.

This achievement was particularly sweet for Connolly as she successfully defended her title, showcasing dominance throughout the tournament. In the championship clash, she bested fellow American, Louise Brough, with a decisive scoreline of 6–2, 7–5. The competition was fierce, with eight seeds and a draw of 96 competitors vying for the prestigious title. But it was Connolly who stood out, continuing her reign at Wimbledon. Her journey to the finals

Maureen Connolly

saw her effortlessly dispatch top contenders, reinforcing her place as a tennis legend in Wimbledon history.

Peter Thomson with his wife Lois, celebrating the victory

Thomson Clinches British Open Glory - July 9th

In the picturesque setting of Royal Birkdale Golf Club, Southport, England, the 90th Open Championship unfolded dramatically. Peter Thomson, a prodigious 23-year-old golfer, secured his maiden Open title, narrowly beating Bobby Locke, Dai Rees, and Syd Scott. This championship was the inaugural event at Royal Birkdale. Over the tournament, players like Sam King and Bill Spence set course records, only to see them broken again. In a captivating final, Thomson displayed exceptional skill, pulling off strategic recoveries and managing a total of 283, surpassing his competitors. This victory, initiated Thomson's remarkable run in the Open Championships, marking him as a golf icon.

Chataway Shatters 5000m Record in London Showdown - October 13th

In an electrifying clash at the White City athletics stadium, West London, 23-year-old Chris Chataway shattered the 5,000 metres world record, finishing at a phenomenal 13 mins 51.6 secs. In a race described as one of Britain's

Chataway and Kuts

finest, Chataway exhibited relentless tenacity against European champion Vladimir Kuts. Kuts dominated most of the race, but Chataway, learning from their prior matchup in Berne, clung fiercely, never trailing by more than a meter. As 40,000 spectators chanted his name and millions watched via a live Eurovision link-up, Chataway summoned unparalleled strength in the final moments, besting the Russian in a heart-pounding finish. Despite Moscow's overall triumph, this unforgettable duel stole the limelight.

International Sports

The first-ever Soviet ice hockey national team

Ice Hockey World Champs: Soviets Ice Out Competition - March 7th

In the Ice Hockey World Championships held in Stockholm, the Soviet Union made an impressive debut. Competing for the first time in the championships, the USSR team displayed unparalleled skill and strategy. Vsevolod Bobrov, a standout player, was honored as the best forward, marking the inauguration of the Directorate Awards. Their journey to gold saw them conquer five matches leading to a critical showdown against the host nation, Sweden. Even though Sweden hoped for redemption following their previous 8-0 loss to Canada, they could only manage a 1-1 tie against the Soviets. The tournament's climax was the face-off between the USSR and Canada's East York Lyndhursts. Contrary to expectations, the Soviets displayed unmatched talent, triumphing 7-2. This victory not only signaled their dominance but also sparked a long-standing hockey rivalry with Canada.

West Germany: FIFA World Cup Champs - July 4th

The fifth FIFA World Cup unfolded with a captivating underdog tale as West Germany triumphed in a nail-biting final against Hungary.

West Germany wrote itself into history

The Hungarian team, a crowd favorite with an impressive 32-match unbeaten run, initially dominated. Yet, the West Germans rallied, flipping a two-goal deficit into a 3-2 victory. This stunning reversal in the Swiss capital, Bern, turned the German squad from underdogs to legends, forever remembered as "The Miracle of Bern." The event was marked not just by this iconic match but also by a high-scoring battle where Austria triumphed over Switzerland. Adding to the intrigue, the German team, equipped with Adi Dassler's innovative studs for the wet conditions, overcame not only their opponents but also swirling controversies of refereeing and doping allegations, securing their place in football lore.

Fangio Speeds to Formula One Championship Title - September 5th

In the eighth season of FIA Formula One, Juan Manuel Fangio claimed the championship, winning races for both Maserati and Mercedes-Benz. This accomplishment marked him as the only driver to win the title for multiple teams in a single season. Argentina's motorsport skill was evident, with José Froilán González securing second place.

Juan Manuel Fangio, Grand Prix de France, 1954

1954 also heralded Mercedes' impactful return to Formula One, after a hiatus post-World War II, introducing the innovative Mercedes-Benz W196. Fangio, having secured initial victories with Maserati, switched to Mercedes, furthering his success. Reigning champion Alberto Ascari, however, faced challenges after moving from Ferrari to Lancia, missing numerous races due to car readiness.

The season was clouded by sorrow as Onofre Marimón tragically perished during the German Grand Prix's practice, casting a shadow on the sporting world.

Chapter V: General 1954

Pop Culture

Bill Haley's Comets Kicks Off Rock Revolution - April 12th

Bill Haley and his Comets perform onstage in New York

Bill Haley & His Comets forever changed the musical landscape by recording "Rock Around the Clock." The band, originally formed in 1947, had already gained attention with "Crazy Man, Crazy," a unique mix of R&B, western, and pop. This song hinted at the emerging rock'n'roll era, and some even consider it the first rock'n'roll song to hit pop charts. However, it was "Rock Around the Clock" that solidified their place in history, becoming one of the best-selling rock singles. Under producer Milt Gabler's guidance, Haley and his band fused musical styles, laying the groundwork for the rock revolution.

Elvis Presley

Elvis: The King's Debut Recording - July 5th

In a defining moment for music, a young Elvis Presley stepped into Sun Records in Memphis, Tennessee, recording the track "That's All Right." This session, which ignited Elvis's unparalleled career, later contributed to his debut studio album released by RCA Victor. This groundbreaking album, a blend of various recording sessions, stormed to the top of the

Billboard Top Pop Albums chart, marking it as the first rock and roll album to achieve this feat. Its legacy persisted, receiving accolades over the decades and cementing Elvis's title as the undisputed "King of Rock 'n' Roll."

'Fellowship of the Ring': Middle-Earth Magic Unleashed - July 29th

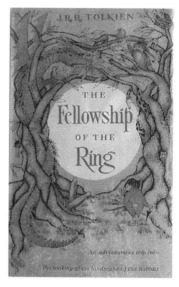

"The Fellowship of the Ring" marks the first volume in J. R. R. Tolkien's epic trilogy, "The Lord of the Rings." It transports readers into the mesmerizing universe of Middle-earth, paving the way for subsequent volumes "The Two Towers" and "The Return of the King." The book masterfully oscillates between moments of tranquility in "Homely Houses" and impending threats, establishing a rhythm of comfort and danger. Its unique narrative structure has

The Fellowship of the Ring

captivated both scholars and critics. Chapters like "The Shadow of the Past" and "The Council of Elrond" deviate from traditional action, offering deep insights through flashbacks.

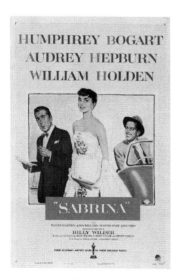

Sabrina

Hepburn's 'Sabrina' Glow Lights Up Screens - September 22nd

"Sabrina," also known as "Sabrina Fair/La Vie en Rose" in the United Kingdom, is a captivating American romantic comedy-drama. The script is adapted from Taylor's play, "Sabrina Fair." Starring the indomitable trio of Humphrey Bogart, Audrey Hepburn, and William Holden, the film narrates the transformative journey of Sabrina Fairchild, the chauffeur's daughter, who returns from Paris a sophisticated woman, turning the lives of the affluent Larrabee brothers upside down.

The famous "flying skirt" image

Monroe's Breezy Moment: Iconic Skirt Takes Flight - September 15th

Marilyn Monroe's iconic moment on a New York subway grate, wearing a white dress fighting the upward breeze, became one of cinema's most memorable scenes from "The Seven Year Itch." While audiences adored the breezy spectacle, this seemingly simple shot had significant personal repercussions for Monroe, notably contributing to tensions in her marriage. Her then-husband, Joe DiMaggio, disapproved of the scene, viewing it as "exhibitionist." Their ensuing public fallout culminated in Monroe filing for divorce, citing "mental cruelty."

Theatrical Release Poster, 1954

Tokyo Roars: Godzilla's Grand Entrance - November 3rd

"Godzilla," introduced the world to the kaiju genre in 1954. This Japanese epic initiated the expansive Godzilla franchise. The film tells of Japan grappling with a colossal monster whose presence stirs nuclear fears in post-war society. Influenced by a canceled Japanese-Indonesian project, its creation story involves a shift from an octopus concept to a dinosaur-like creature. With unique special effects, notably "suitmation", the film took months to shoot. While its initial reception was mixed, "Godzilla" became an international cultural icon, spawning sequels, and establishing a benchmark for tokusatsu media.

 Most Popular Books from 1954 (goodreads.com)

* "The Fellowship of the Ring" (The Lord of the Rings, #1) by J.R.R. Tolkien

* "Lord of the Flies" by William Golding

* "The Two Towers" (The Lord of the Rings, #2) by J.R.R. Tolkien

* "The Horse and His Boy" (Chronicles of Narnia, #5) by C.S. Lewis

* "Live and Let Die" (James Bond, #2) by Ian Fleming

* "Katherine" by Anya Seton

* "Horton Hears a Who!" by Dr. Seuss

* "Lucky Jim" by Kingsley Amis

* "A Child's Christmas in Wales" by Dylan Thomas

* "The Wonderful Flight to the Mushroom Planet" (The Mushroom Planet, #1) by Eleanor Cameron

* "The Matchmaker" by Thornton Wilder

* "Beyond the Hundredth Meridian: John Wesley Powell and the Second Opening of the West" by Wallace Stegner

* "The Doors of Perception and Heaven and Hell" by Aldous Huxley

Technological Advancements

Georgetown-IBM: Machine Translation's NY Debut - January 7th

The first public demonstration of a machine translation system held in New York at the head office of IBM

The Georgetown-IBM machine translation demonstration was an early foray into computer-assisted language translation, using a basic system on an IBM 701 mainframe. The setup, with a scant six grammar rules and a 250-word lexicon from various disciplines, showcased the potential of technology in overcoming language barriers. Originating from a 1952 MIT conference idea, the demonstration translated over 60 carefully selected Russian sentences into English. This process involved encoding Russian words into numbers and then converting them into English, demonstrating a 'lexicographical' approach. Despite its simplicity, this event marked a significant milestone in the field of computational linguistics and machine learning.

USS Nautilus Dives In: Nuke-Sub Era Begins - January 21st

The USS Nautilus ushered in the nuclear submarine era, revolutionizing underwater naval capabilities with its 1954 launch. Its nuclear power allowed for unprecedented, submerged endurance, outperforming traditional diesel-electric submarines. Commanded by Eugene Wilkinson, the vessel's design informed future submarine construction. Its 1958 polar transit stands as a

The world's first nuclear submarine

remarkable accomplishment. After decommissioning in 1980, the Nautilus earned National Historic Landmark status. It now serves as a museum in Connecticut, attracting numerous visitors yearly. The Nautilus' reactor not only set the standard for American nuclear subs but also impacted global naval propulsion.

Bell Labs' Solar Revolution: Phototransistor Unveiled - April 25th

Bell Laboratories pioneered the first practical silicon solar cell, drawing inspiration from Becquerel's 1839 discovery of the photovoltaic effect. For years, researchers tested selenium for solar purposes, but its efficiency remained below 1%. In the 1940s, a breakthrough at Bell Labs saw Russell Ohl accidentally produce a pivotal p-n junction for solar cells. Building on this, Daryl Chapin, Calvin Fuller, and Gerald Pearson collaborated to develop an impressive 6% efficient cell.

Installation of the first successful solar panel and solar battery, for the Georgia telephone carrier Americus

Branded as the "solar battery", it powered both a toy and a radio transmitter, capturing public fascination. This significant advancement laid the foundation for today's solar technologies that boast efficiencies of over 40%.

Obninsk Powers Up: World's First Nuclear Station - June 27th

The World's First Nuclear Power Plant

Obninsk Nuclear Power Plant, located in the "Science City" of Obninsk, was a pioneering establishment in the field of nuclear energy. About 110 km southwest of Moscow, this facility made history as the world's first grid-connected nuclear power plant. Commissioned in 1954, Obninsk marked the beginning of an era where nuclear reactors produced electricity on an industrial scale, although its scale was relatively modest. While its primary function was electricity generation until 1959, the plant later pivoted to research and isotope production. Insights from experimental studies at Obninsk laid the foundation for the development of larger RBMK reactors. Its impactful 48-year operation was notable for its safety record, with no significant incidents or environmental contamination.

Radio Revolution: Texas Instruments' Transistor Triumph - October 18th

The landscape of modern electronics was forever altered with the transistor's introduction, a key component in devices. While the concept of a transistor was initially proposed by physicist Julius Edgar Lilienfeld in 1926, it took another two decades until the first functional device was created by John

Bardeen, Walter Brattain, and
William Shockley at Bell Labs in
1947. Their groundbreaking work
earned them a Nobel Prize in
Physics. Texas Instruments took
this innovation further when they
collaborated with Regency Division
of I.D.E.A. to unveil the Regency
TR-1, the first production-model
pocket transistor radio, in 1954.
Crafted in Indianapolis, this nearly

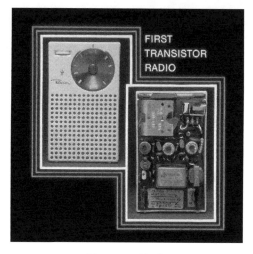

FIRST
TRANSISTOR
RADIO

Transistor Radio

pocket-sized marvel came in an array of colors, symbolizing the fusion of
technological prowess and design aesthetics.

Dr. Murray's Medical Feat: First Kidney Transplant Done - December 23rd

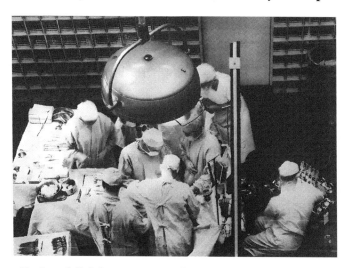

Dr. Joseph E. Murray, at center facing camera, performing the
first successful organ transplant

Dr. Joseph Edward
Murray achieved a
medical milestone by
performing the first
successful human
kidney transplant.
The landmark
surgery involved
identical twins, with
Richard Herrick
receiving a kidney
to treat his chronic

nephritis. Conducted by Murray and his team over five hours at Peter Bent
Brigham Hospital, the operation laid the groundwork for future transplants.
Murray's work revolutionized the field with pioneering allografts, cadaveric

transplants, and the use of immunosuppressive drugs. His dedication significantly advanced organ transplantation, earning him the Nobel Prize in Physiology or Medicine in 1990 for these life-saving innovations.

Fashion

The 1950s stood as a period post-war and pre-revolution, where the lines between tradition and rebellion began to blur. This era saw the crescendo of cinema's golden age, projecting larger-than-life icons onto the global stage, while fashion houses in the bustling streets of Paris,

1954 Men's Fall Sport Coats

Milan, London, and New York reimagined the garments of men and women alike.

Elvis Wearing a Hawaiian Shirt

The 1950s was a time when men's clothing epitomized a blend of formality and casual relaxation. Sharp suits, slim ties, and polished shoes set the standard for the business realm. Yet, beyond the corporate arena, casual wear saw a surge in popularity. Hawaiian shirts, influenced by America's increased interest in the Pacific post-WWII, burst onto the scene. Cardigans and loafers became wardrobe staples for the weekend warrior.

James Dean: Defining 1950s Fashion Elegance

Still, in the backdrop of these shifts was the rebellious greaser look: leather jackets, rolled-up denim, and slick-backed hair, inspired by the likes of James Dean and Marlon Brando. This duality showcased a generation of men standing on the brink of change, straddling the boundary between wartime restraint and the looming freedom of the '60s.

For women, the '50s danced between elegance and audacity. The decade began with the tightened waists and voluminous skirts of Dior's "New Look", celebrating a return to opulence after the wartime years. But alongside these luxurious designs, practicality played a role too. Capri pants, for instance, became popularized during this period, offering women a comfortable yet chic alternative.

The twinset, a matching sweater and cardigan combo, was another favorite, signaling a blend of sophistication and ease. Icons like Marilyn Monroe and Audrey Hepburn showcased sleeker, more form-fitting silhouettes, representing a shift in societal perspectives about femininity and sensuality. Accessories also took center stage with pearls becoming a staple, often associated with the class and refinement of Jacqueline Kennedy.

The New Look by Christian Dior

Capri Pants

Twinset

Jacqueline Kennedy: The Epitome
of Class and Style

In the '50s, cinema's influence on
fashion was undeniable. This wasn't
merely a golden age for movies; film
became a powerful medium shaping
global fashion trends. Hollywood's
glamour seeped into wardrobes,
while international films, especially
from Europe, introduced audiences
to French elegance and Italian chic.
Television, a new entrant into homes,
amplified this influence by bringing
iconic movie styles and film stars
directly to viewers, creating immediate
cultural touchpoints.

Cars

The mid-1950s saw the American auto industry transform with advanced post-war tech like the overhead-valve V8 engine. The Big Three automakers – General Motors, Ford, and Chrysler – commanded a 94% market share, overshadowing independent carmakers. In a move emblematic of the times, Hudson and Nash-Kelvinator merged, creating the American Motors Corporation (AMC), reflecting a broader consolidation trend. Meanwhile, Studebaker and Packard, once industry forerunners, united, highlighting the smaller companies' struggle to compete with dominant industry players.

Top Selling Cars

U.S.A

1954 Chevrolet Bel Air

1954 Ford Crestline Sunliner

Chevrolet's Bel Air epitomized the American dream on wheels. Its chrome details, colorful two-tone designs, and powerful performance set it apart. With sales reaching 1,150,000 units, it embodied the spirit of the age. A significant part of its appeal was the introduction of the first V8 engine since the 1910s by Chevrolet, enhancing its appeal among car enthusiasts.

The Ford Crestline Sunliner was another standout, with its convertible top and V8 engine. Ford managed to sell approximately 1,165,000 units, putting up stiff competition to Chevrolet. The Sunliner was known for its sleek design, complemented by chrome detailing and a distinctive bullet nose.

U.K.

Morris Minor, the classic British car, saw its popularity soar in 1954. With sales reaching around 100,000 units, it became a symbol of British motor engineering. Compact yet spacious, the Minor was both economical and stylish, making it a favorite for families and city dwellers.

1954 Morris Minor

Another British favorite was the Austin A30, which competed closely with the Morris Minor. With a sales figure of roughly 90,000 units in that year, the A30 was appreciated for its affordable price, durability, and its modern design. Its compact size made it perfect for narrow British streets, while its efficient engine was economical on fuel.

1954 Austin A30

Fastest Car

In 1954, two remarkable sports cars captured the world's attention. The Jaguar D-Type, explicitly crafted for the Le Mans 24-hour race,

1954 Jaguar D-Type

demonstrated a blend of speed and innovation. With its aeronautical-inspired monocoque structure and a signature vertical stabilizer, it housed a 3.4L straight-6 XK engine, dashing from 0-60 mph (0-97 km/h) in a breathtaking 4.7 seconds. This racing marvel even transitioned to the streets, with certain models morphing into the road legal XKSS versions.

The Mercedes-Benz 300 SL Gullwing Coupe, stemming from the 1952 W194 race car, stood out with its iconic gull-wing doors and light build. Its advanced straight-six engine propelled it to 163 mph (262 km/h), making it the swiftest production car of its

1954 Mercedes-Benz 300 SL Gullwing Coupe

time. Brought to the U.S. by importer Max Hoffman, the 300 SL became a classic, revered for blending speed, design, and technological ingenuity.

Most Expensive American Car of 1954

In the realm of luxury, the Cadillac Eldorado Convertible was the showstopper in 1954. With a staggering price of $5,738, it was the pinnacle of opulence. The Eldorado was adorned with a golden crest, whitewall tires, and a parade

1954 Cadillac Eldorado Convertible

boot, indicating its elite status. Its interior displayed luxury finishes and top-of-the-line technology for the time. The combination of power and luxury made it the preferred choice for the affluent.

Most Powerful Muscle Car of 1954

Before the term "muscle car" became popular, powerful performance cars were making waves, and the Chrysler C-300 led the pack in that year. Termed as the "Businessman's Hot Rod," the C-300 featured 300

1954 Chrysler C-300

horsepower, courtesy of its Hemi V8 engine. Although the muscle car era's golden years were still a decade away, the C-300 was a clear precursor, showcasing raw power combined with a sleek design. With dual exhausts, a performance camshaft, and solid lifters, it set the stage for the high-performance vehicles of the future.

Popular Recreation

1954 was a remarkable year in the realm of popular recreation, marked by the influence of several noteworthy events. As the post-war era moved forward, technology, culture, and economic landscapes significantly impacted the world of leisure, defining the year's favorite pastimes.

One influential figure who began to change the music scene and youth culture was Elvis Presley. As he started his legendary career in this year with hits like "That's All Right," his music became a sensation almost overnight. The charismatic singer introduced a unique blend of rhythm, blues, and rock 'n' roll that soon made its way into the transistor radios of many.

Elvis in 1954

Elvis didn't just bring new music; he introduced a new way of life, dance, and fashion. His infectious energy and groundbreaking style began to dominate teen gatherings, from diners to soda shops, where the latest Elvis hits played on jukeboxes, fueling the spirit of rebellion and transformation.

Matchbox Cars continued their dominant reign in children's play, captivating imaginations with their miniature representations. However, an iconic toy that would shape generations was born in Europe – LEGO. The initial Automatic Binding Brick sets, such as the Gaveæske, were more than just building bricks. Introduced in 1949 with sets like 700/1, 700/2, and 700/3, these bricks were available in Red, White, Yellow, Light Green,

Matchbox Car

LEGO set 700/3A

and sometimes Medium Blue. Interestingly, the early versions of these bricks even included slots to hold postcards or pictures, enabling children to craft their picture frames. By 1954, LEGO introduced a new series of windows with glass panes, hinting at the limitless building possibilities that lay ahead.

In the technological forefront, the transistor radio emerged as a game-changer. While not merely a child's plaything, its introduction significantly impacted youthful entertainment. These pocket-sized wonders became instruments of revolution, granting the younger generation a newfound musical freedom and independence.

The Transistor Radio

But the year also had its share of quirky innovations. Enter Mr. Potato Head, a toy that would become a household name. Created by George Lerner in 1949, it was Hasbro that brought it to the masses in 1952. This playful toy made history as the first to be advertised on television, targeting children directly.

Vintage 1950s Mr. Potato Head kit

By 1953, the Potato Head family expanded, introducing Mrs. Potato Head, Brother Spud, and Sister Yam. Reflecting the era's affluence, the toy line even included a car, boat trailer, kitchen set, stroller, and pets.

Mr. Potato Head 1954 Hasbro Print Ad

Among these innovations, classic outdoor games kept their appeal. Children continued to find joy in hopscotch, skipping ropes, hula hoops, and marbles, turning streets and playgrounds into realms of endless possibilities. Collectibles, like trading cards and cereal box toys, added a touch of excitement to daily routines.

The trend of watching films at drive-in theaters persisted, offering a unique mix of entertainment and social interaction.

For teenagers and adults, the culture of gathering at diners and soda shops remained a hallmark of the times.

From innovative toys to emerging technologies and classic pastimes, this year showcased a blend of tradition and forward-thinking. It was an era that celebrated the simple pleasures of life while paving the way for future innovations in recreation.

Mr. B's Hamburgers, 1954

Chapter VI: Births & Deaths 1954

Births (onthisday.com)

January 12th – Howard Stern: American Radio Personality

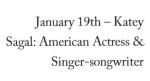
January 19th – Katey Sagal: American Actress & Singer-songwriter

January 29th – Oprah Winfrey: American TV Host and Actress

February 15th – Matt Groening: American Cartoonist and Writer

February 17th – Rene Russo: American Model and Actress

February 18th – John Travolta: American Actor

February 20th – Patty Hearst: American Philanthropist and Kidnap Victim

February 23rd – Viktor Yushchenko: Ukrainian Politician

February 26th – Recep Tayyip Erdoğan: Turkish Politician

March 4th – Catherine O'Hara: Canadian Actress

April 7th – Jackie Chan: Hong Kong Martial Artist and Actor

April 9th – Dennis Quaid: American Actor

April 23rd – Michael Moore: American Filmmaker

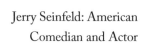

Jerry Seinfeld: American Comedian and Actor

Jane Campion: New Zealand Film Director

Andre Dawson: American Baseball Hall of Famer

Angela Merkel: German Politician

Vitas Gerulaitis: American Tennis Player

Hugo Chávez: Former Venezuelan President

August 12th – François Hollande: French Politician

August 15th – Stieg Larsson: Swedish Author

August 16th – James Cameron: Canadian Film Director

August 25th – Elvis Costello: English Singer-songwriter

August 30th – Alexander Lukashenko: Belarusian President

September 20th – Lloyd Blankfein: American CEO of Goldman Sachs

September 21st – Shinzō Abe: Former Japanese Prime Minister

October 3rd – Al Sharpton: American Minister and Activist

October 3rd – Stevie Ray Vaughan: American Blues Guitarist

 October 10th – David Lee Roth: American Rock Singer

October 29th – Lee Child (James Grant): English Author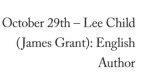

 November 8th – Kazuo Ishiguro: British Author

November 14th – Condoleezza Rice: Former U.S. Secretary of State

 December 18th – Ray Liotta: American Actor

December 21st – Chris Evert: American Tennis Player

 December 25th – Annie Lennox: Scottish Singer-songwriter

December 28th – Denzel Washington: American Actor

Deaths (onthisday.com)

 January 18th – Sydney Greenstreet: British-American Actor

February 1st – Edwin Howard Armstrong: American Electrical Engineer & Inventor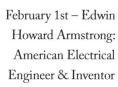

 February 13th – Agnes Macphail: Ontario Parliament Member

April 3rd – Aristides de Sousa Mendes: Portuguese Diplomat

 April 4th – Pierre S. du Pont: American Entrepreneur

May 19th – Charles Ives: American Composer

May 24th – William Van Alen: American Architect

May 25th – Robert Capa: Hungarian–American War Photographer

June 7th – Alan Turing: English mathematician, Computer Scientist, Logician, Cryptanalyst

July 13th – Grantland Rice: American Sportswriter

July 13th – Frida Kahlo: Mexican Painter

July 24th – Mary Church Terrell: American Civil Rights Activist

August 3rd – Colette: French Author

September 4th – The French Angel: Russian-born French Professional Wrestler

September 7th – Pop Warner: American Football Coach

September 8th – André Derain: French Artist & Co-founder of Fauvism

November 3rd – Henri Matisse: French Visual Artist & Co-founder of Fauvism

November 15th – Lionel Barrymore: American Actor & Director

November 28th – Enrico Fermi: Italian Physicist (later naturalized American)

December 8th – Claude Cahun: French Surrealist Photographer

December 8th – Gladys George: American Actress

December 30th – Günther Quandt: German Industrialist

Chapter VII: Statistics 1954

* U.S. GDP 1954 – $390.5 billion USD (countryeconomy.com)

* U.S. GDP 2022 – 25.46 trillion USD (worldbank.org)

* U.K. GDP 1954 – 48.1 billion USD (worldbank.org)

* U.K. GDP 2022 – 3.07 trillion USD (worldbank.org)

* U.S. Inflation 1954 – 3.54% (dollartimes.com)

* U.S. Inflation 2022 – 8.0% (worldbank.org)

* U.K. Inflation 1954 – 1.98% (officialdata.org)

* U.K. Inflation 2022 – 7.9% (worldbank.org)

* U.S. Population 1954 – 158,205,873 (macrotrends.net)

* U.S. Population 2022 - 333,287,557 (worldbank.org)

* U.K. Population 1954 – 50,969,939 (macrotrends.net)

* U.K. Population 2022 - 66,971.41 (worldbank.org)

* U.S. Life Expectancy at Birth 1954 – 68.90 (macrotrends.net)

* U.S. Life Expectancy at Birth 2022 - 79.05 (macrotrends.net)

* U.K. Life Expectancy at Birth 1954 – 69.65 (macrotrends.net)

* U.K. Life Expectancy at Birth 2022 – 81.65 (macrotrends.net)

* U.S. Annual Working Hours Per Worker 1954 - 1,997 (ourworldindata.org)

* U.S. Annual Working Hours Per Worker 2017 - 1,757 (ourworldindata.org)

* U.K. Annual Working Hours Per Worker 1954 - 2,169

* (ourworldindata.org)

* U.K. Annual Working Hours Per Worker 2017 - 1,670

* (ourworldindata.org)

* U.S. Unemployment Rate 1954 – 5.0% (thebalancemoney.com)

* U.S. Unemployment Rate 2022 – 3.6% (worldbank.org)

* U.K. Unemployment Rate 1954 - 1.77% (fred.stlouisfed.org)

* U.K. Unemployment Rate 2022 – 3.7% (ons.gov.uk)

* U.S. Tax Revenue (% of GDP) 1954 – 17.85% (worldbank.org)

* U.S. Tax Revenue (% of GDP) 2021 – 11.2% (worldbank.org)

* U.K. Tax Revenue (% of GDP) 1954 – 40.73% (ceicdata.com)

* U.K. Tax Revenue (% of GDP) 2021 – 26.4% (worldbank.org)

* U.S. Prison Population 1954 – 274,819 (bjs.ojp.gov)

* U.S. Prison Population 2021 - 1,204,300 (bjs.ojp.gov)

* U.K. Prison Population 1954 - 24,735 (parliament.uk)

* U.K. Prison Population 2022 - 81,806 (gov.uk)

* U.S. Average Cost of a New House 1954 – $10,250 (doyouremember.com)

* U.S. Average Cost of a New House 2022 – $454,900 (gobankingrates.com)

* U.K. Average Cost of a New House 1954 – £1,863 (retrowow.co.uk)

* U.K. Average Cost of a New House 2022 – £296,000 (ons.gov.uk)

* U.S. Average Income per Year 1954 – $4,200 (census.gov)

* U.S. Average Income per Year US – $56,368 (demandsage.com)

* U.K. Average Income per Year 1954 – £512,00 (gov.uk)

* U.K. Average Income per Year 2022 – £33,000 (gov.uk)

* U.S. Cost of Living: The $100 from 1954 has grown to about $1,141.36 today, up $1,041.36 over 69 years due to an average yearly inflation of 3.59%, resulting in a 1,041.36% total price hike (in2013dollars.com).

* U.K. Cost of Living: Today's £3,503.03 mirrors the purchasing power of £100 in 1954, showing a £3,403.03 hike over 69 years. The pound's yearly inflation rate averaged 5.23% over this period, leading to a 3,403.03% total price rise (in2013dollars.com).

Cost of Things

United States

* Men's suit, dacron: $60.00 (mclib.info)

* Women's dress, cotton-orlon: $8.98 (mclib.info)

* Women's handbags: $5.32-$16.67 (mclib.info)

* Fresh eggs (1 dozen): $.61 (kltv.com)

* White bread (1 pound): $.15 (mclib.info)

* Sliced bacon (1 pound): $.87 (mclib.info)

* Round steak (1 pound): $.61 (mclib.info)

* Potatoes (10 pounds): $.53 (kltv.com)

* Fresh grocery milk (1/2 gallon): $.43 (kltv.com)

* Price per gallon (Gas): $.23 (kltv.com)

* Coffee (1 pound): $.93 (kltv.com)

* Tuna (6 ½ oz. can): $.25 (kltv.com)

* Oreo cookies (11¾ oz. pkg): $.39 (kltv.com)

United Kingdom (retrowow.co.uk)

* Gallon of petrol: 4s 6½d

* Pint of beer: 1s 10d (bottled)

* 20 cigarettes: 3s 7d

* Loaf of bread (white, unwrapped): 7½d

* Loose leaf tea 4oz: 1s 7¼d

* Sugar 1lb: 7½d

* Pint of milk: 7d

* Butter ½lb: 1s 10½d

* Cheddar cheese 1lb: 2s ½d

* Margarine 1lb: 1s 9d

* Eggs 1 dozen: 4s

* Potatoes lb: 2d

* Onions lb: 4¼d

* Oranges lb: 1s

* Coal - 1cwt: 5s 9d

* Ferranti 17" television: 75 guineas

* Qualcast Commando power lawn mower: £29 15s

* The Daily Mirror newspaper: 1½d

* Astral refrigerator: £44 18s

* Hoover washing machine: £46 2s 8d

Chapter VIII: Iconic Advertisements of 1954

IBM Electric Typewriters

Martini & Rossi

Lucky Strike

Lustre-Creme Shampoo

Quaker Oats

Regency Pocket Radio

7 Up

Camels

Colgate Dental Cream with Gardol

General Electric Spacemaker

Smirnoff Vodka

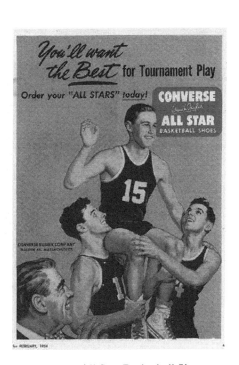

Converse All Star Basketball Shoes

United Airlines

Campbell's Soups

Palmolive Soap

1954 Ford Lincoln

Coca-Cola

Philips Radios

Dickies

Northwest Orient Airlines

Kellogg's Corn Flakes

Tide

1954 Plymouth

Marlboro

Budweiser

Kodak Brownie Movie Camera

Chesterfield

1954 Chevrolet

Firestone Tyres

I have a gift for you!

Dear reader, thank you so much for reading my book!

To make this book more (much more!) affordable, all images are in black and white, but I've created a special gift for you!

You can now have access, for FREE, to the PDF version of this book with the original images!

Keep in mind that some are originally black and white, but some are colored.

I hope you enjoy it!

Download it here:

bit.ly/3V8YYVM

Or Scan this QR Code:

I have a favor to ask you!

I deeply hope you've enjoyed reading this book and felt transported right into 1954!

I loved researching it, organizing it, and writing it, knowing that it would make your day a little brighter.

If you've enjoyed it too, I would be extremely grateful if you took just a few minutes to leave a positive customer review and share it with your friends.

As an unknown author, that makes all the difference and gives me the extra energy I need to keep researching, writing, and bringing joy to all my readers. Thank you!

Best regards,
David J. Anderson

Please leave a positive book review here:

amzn.to/3t3N9Ey

Or Scan this QR Code:

Discover All the Books in This Collection!

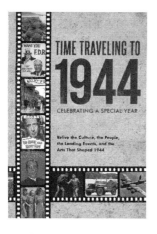
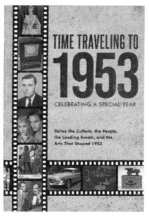

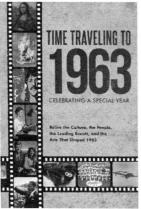
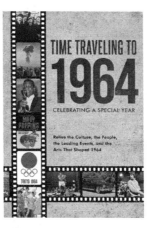

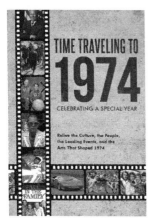
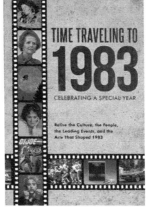
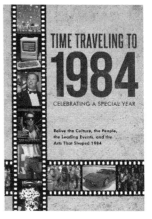

Made in the USA
Las Vegas, NV
27 October 2024

10501982R10059